BREAKING BOUNDARIES: HOW TECHNOLOGY IS CHANGING THE GAME

THE GAME-CHANGING POTENTIAL OF TECHNOLOGY: ARE YOU READY TO PLAY

TIRTH PATEL

AF565476

Copyright © Tirth Patel
All Rights Reserved.

This book has been self-published with all reasonable efforts taken to make the material error-free by the author. No part of this book shall be used, reproduced in any manner whatsoever without written permission from the author, except in the case of brief quotations embodied in critical articles and reviews.

The Author of this book is solely responsible and liable for its content including but not limited to the views, representations, descriptions, statements, information, opinions and references ["Content"]. The Content of this book shall not constitute or be construed or deemed to reflect the opinion or expression of the Publisher or Editor. Neither the Publisher nor Editor endorse or approve the Content of this book or guarantee the reliability, accuracy or completeness of the Content published herein and do not make any representations or warranties of any kind, express or implied, including but not limited to the implied warranties of merchantability, fitness for a particular purpose. The Publisher and Editor shall not be liable whatsoever for any errors, omissions, whether such errors or omissions result from negligence, accident, or any other cause or claims for loss or damages of any kind, including without limitation, indirect or consequential loss or damage arising out of use, inability to use, or about the reliability, accuracy or sufficiency of the information contained in this book.

Made with ❤ on the Notion Press Platform
www.notionpress.com

To all the pioneers, innovators, and disruptors who have dared to challenge convention and push the boundaries of what is possible with technology. Your vision, creativity, and determination have paved the way for a brighter future, and your contributions have touched the lives of countless people around the world. This book is dedicated to you, with gratitude and admiration for all that you have accomplished, and all that you continue to inspire.

Contents

Foreword

Technology is transforming our world at an unprecedented pace, challenging us to adapt and innovate in ways that were once unimaginable. From artificial intelligence and machine learning to blockchain and the Internet of Things, emerging technologies are breaking down barriers and unlocking new possibilities in virtually every industry and sector.

In "Breaking Boundaries: How Technology is Changing the Game", we explore the cutting-edge of innovation and disruption, offering insights and inspiration for anyone looking to stay ahead of the curve. Through stories of pioneering individuals and companies, as well as analysis of emerging trends and developments, this book provides a comprehensive guide to navigating the changing landscape of technology.

More than just a catalog of tech trends, "Breaking Boundaries" is a call to action for leaders, entrepreneurs, and changemakers everywhere. By embracing the potential of technology and daring to challenge convention, we can build a better future for ourselves and for generations to come.

It is my honor to introduce this book, and to invite you to join us on a journey of discovery, inspiration, and transformation.

[Tirth Patel]

Preface

As someone who has spent my career at the intersection of technology and business, I have had a front-row seat to some of the most exciting developments of the past few decades. From the early days of the internet to the rise of artificial intelligence and beyond, I have seen firsthand the transformative power of innovation and disruption.

But as much as I have learned over the years, I am constantly reminded of how much there is still to discover. Technology is advancing at an unprecedented pace, and the implications of these changes are far-reaching and complex. In many ways, we are still only scratching the surface of what is possible.

That's why I wrote this book. "Breaking Boundaries: How Technology is Changing the Game" is my attempt to capture some of the most important trends, developments, and insights that are shaping the future of technology. Through a series of stories and analyses, I hope to provide readers with a comprehensive understanding of the forces that are driving innovation and disruption, and the implications of these changes for society, business, and beyond.

Of course, this book is not meant to be the final word on the subject. Technology is constantly evolving, and the ideas and perspectives that I share here will no doubt be outdated in the not-too-distant future. But I hope that this book will serve as a valuable starting point for those who want to explore the cutting-edge of technology and stay ahead of the curve.

So without further ado, I invite you to join me on this journey of discovery and exploration. Together, let's break down boundaries and unlock the incredible potential of technology for a better future.

[Tirth Patel]

Acknowledgements

Writing a book is a collaborative effort, and there are many people who have contributed to the creation of "Breaking Boundaries: How Technology is Changing the Game". I would like to take this opportunity to express my gratitude to the following individuals:

First and foremost, I want to thank my family and loved ones for their unwavering support and encouragement throughout the writing process. Your belief in me and my work has meant the world to me.

I also want to thank my colleagues and friends in the technology and business communities, who have provided me with invaluable insights and feedback on the ideas presented in this book. Your expertise and perspectives have been instrumental in shaping my thinking.

I am also grateful to the many pioneers, innovators, and disruptors who have blazed a trail in the world of technology, and whose stories and achievements have inspired me to write this book. Your contributions to the field are immeasurable, and I hope that this book does justice to your vision and impact.

Last but not least, I want to thank the team at [publisher name], who have worked tirelessly to bring this book to life. Your professionalism, dedication, and expertise have made this journey an unforgettable one.

Thank you all, from the bottom of my heart.

[Tirth Patel] Breaking Boundaries: How Technology is Changing the Game

Prologue

Technology has always been a powerful force for change. From the wheel to the printing press to the internet, each new innovation has transformed the way we live, work, and interact with each other. But never before has technology been advancing at such a breakneck pace, with such far-reaching implications for every aspect of our lives.

In this book, "Breaking Boundaries: How Technology is Changing the Game", I aim to explore the frontiers of this technological revolution, to understand the driving forces behind it, and to consider the opportunities and challenges that lie ahead. Through a combination of storytelling and analysis, I will examine the trends and developments that are shaping the future of technology, and explore what they mean for individuals, businesses, and society as a whole.

At its core, this book is a celebration of innovation and disruption. It is a recognition of the power of human ingenuity and creativity, and an acknowledgement of the incredible potential that technology holds to make the world a better place. But it is also a call to action, a challenge to embrace the future with optimism and curiosity, and a reminder that the decisions we make today will shape the world of tomorrow.

So let us embark on this journey together, and let us break down boundaries and push the limits of what is possible. The future is ours to create, and the time to start is now.

[Tirth Patel]

Prologue

CHAPTER ONE

The Tech Wizard

Deep in the heart of Silicon Valley, there was a young computer whiz by the name of Alex. From a young age, Alex had always been fascinated by technology, and spent hours tinkering with gadgets and gizmos in his parents' garage. As he grew older, Alex's passion for tech only intensified. He spent his teenage years studying computer science, coding in his free time, and learning everything he could about the latest breakthroughs in the field. By the time he graduated high school, Alex was already being hailed as a prodigy. But Alex was far from content to rest on his laurels. He knew that the true test of his abilities would be to create something truly groundbreaking - something that could change the world. So he poured all of his energy and creativity into a new project: a revolutionary piece of software that would transform the way people interacted with their computers. For months, he worked tirelessly, barely sleeping or eating, completely consumed by his vision. And then, finally, it was finished. Alex had created a program that was unlike anything anyone had ever seen before. It was intuitive, it was fast, and it was beautiful - a true work of art. But as proud as Alex was of his creation, he knew that he couldn't bring it to market alone. He needed a team of like-minded individuals who shared his vision, who could help him refine his ideas and bring them to life. So he set out to find the best and brightest minds in the tech world - people who were as passionate and driven as he was. He searched high and low, attending conferences and meetups, scouring the internet for potential collaborators.

It wasn't easy. Alex had high standards, and he refused to compromise on the quality of his team. But eventually, he found a group of people who were just as committed to the cause as he was. Together, they worked day and night, polishing Alex's program until it was ready to be released to the world. And the response was overwhelming. People from all over the globe marveled at Alex's creation, praising its elegance and simplicity. It was hailed as a true game-changer, the kind of software that could transform the way people interacted with their technology. For Alex, it was the ultimate validation. He had poured his heart and soul into this project, and to see it succeed was a dream come true. But he knew that this was only the beginning. There were countless other problems in the world that technology could solve, and Alex was determined to be at the forefront of that change. And so he continued to dream, to innovate, to push the boundaries of what was possible. Because for Alex, the magic of technology was not in what it could do - but in what it could inspire people to do.

CHAPTER TWO

Breaking the Mold: Challenging Convention with Technology

It was a hot day in the middle of summer, and Anna was feeling restless. She had been working as a software engineer for a few years now, and while she enjoyed the work, she couldn't help feeling like something was missing. She had always been drawn to technology because of its potential to change the world. But lately, it seemed like most of the projects she was working on were simply incremental improvements on existing products. There was nothing truly revolutionary about what she was doing.

So Anna decided to take matters into her own hands. She began to research new technologies and innovative ideas, looking for ways to break the mold and challenge convention. One idea in particular caught her eye: virtual reality. It was still a relatively new field, with a lot of potential for growth and experimentation. Anna was convinced that with the right approach, she could create a VR experience that would be truly game-changing. But she knew that she couldn't do it alone. She needed a team of talented people who shared her vision, who were willing to take risks and push the boundaries of what was possible. So Anna began to recruit. She reached out to friends and colleagues, posted on social media, and attended industry events. Slowly but surely, she assembled a team of experts in fields ranging from game design to artificial intelligence. Together, they worked tirelessly to create a virtual reality experience unlike anything anyone had ever seen before. They incorporated cutting-edge technology like haptic feedback and motion tracking, pushing the limits of what was possible. And when they finally unveiled their creation to the world, the response was overwhelming. People were blown away by the sheer scope and imagination of the experience. It was like nothing they had ever seen before - a true breakthrough in the field of virtual reality.

For Anna, it was a vindication of everything she had been striving for. She had challenged convention, taken risks, and broken new ground - all with the help of an incredible team of like-minded individuals. And as she looked out over the sea of smiling faces, all lost in the wonder of her creation, Anna knew that this was only the beginning. There was still so much more she wanted to accomplish, so many more boundaries she wanted to push. But for now, she was content to revel in the joy of having created something truly unique and innovative. Because for Anna, that was what technology was all about - not simply making incremental improvements, but challenging convention and changing the world for the better. Anna's team continued to refine their virtual reality experience, pushing the boundaries of what was possible with each new iteration. They received offers from major tech companies and investors, all eager to get in on the ground floor of this groundbreaking technology. As they continued to innovate, they faced many challenges along the way. There were technical hurdles to overcome, as well as creative roadblocks and even personal conflicts within the team. But through it all, Anna remained focused on her goal: to create something truly revolutionary that would change the world. Months turned into years, and Anna and her team continued to work tirelessly. They created partnerships with other companies and organizations, pooling resources and expertise to take their technology even further. And as they did, they began to see the impact their work was having on the world around them.

Their virtual reality experience was being used to train soldiers, allowing them to experience realistic combat scenarios in a safe and controlled environment. It was being used to help patients with PTSD, allowing them to confront and overcome their fears in a virtual space. And it was being used in education, providing students with immersive and engaging learning experiences that were more effective than traditional classroom methods.

For Anna, it was incredibly rewarding to see the impact her work was having. She had always believed that technology could change the world, but now she was seeing it firsthand. And as she looked back on everything she and her team had accomplished, she knew that they had truly broken the mold and challenged convention.

But even as she celebrated their successes, Anna knew that there was always more work to be done. She and her team continued to push the boundaries of what was possible, exploring new technologies and innovative ideas. And with every breakthrough, they came closer to their ultimate goal: to create a world where technology was used not just to make incremental improvements, but to truly change the world for the better.

As Anna looked to the future, she was filled with hope and excitement. She knew that there would be challenges and setbacks along the way, but she was confident that with the right mindset and a dedication to innovation, anything was possible. And with that, she and her team set out to make their next breakthrough, determined to change the world one innovation at a time.

CHAPTER THREE

The Power of Collaboration: Bridging Disciplines with Technology

As technology continues to evolve at an unprecedented pace, the boundaries between different disciplines are becoming increasingly blurred. Engineers, designers, and artists are working together to create innovative new products and experiences, while scientists and engineers are collaborating to push the boundaries of what we know about the world around us.

At the forefront of this movement is a group of passionate individuals who believe that the key to unlocking the full potential of technology lies in collaboration across disciplines. One such person is Alex, a young engineer who had always been interested in the intersection of art and technology. After finishing his degree in engineering, Alex had worked for a number of different companies, but he had always felt like something was missing. It wasn't until he attended a conference on the future of technology that he realized what it was: he wanted to work with artists to create something truly unique and innovative.

Over the next few years, Alex attended art exhibitions and collaborated with artists to create works that combined engineering with art. Together, they created installations that responded to human movement, sculptures that used technology to create illusions, and even clothing that incorporated sensors and other tech. As Alex continued to work with artists, he began to see the power of collaboration firsthand. By combining different skill sets and perspectives, he and his collaborators were able to create experiences that were greater than the sum of their parts. And as they shared their work with others, they found that it was inspiring others to think outside the box and break down the traditional boundaries between disciplines. For Alex, the power of collaboration was clear. By working together, he and his collaborators were able to create something truly unique and innovative, pushing the boundaries of what was possible with technology and art.

CHAPTER FOUR

The Ethics of Innovation: Navigating the Risks and Rewards of New Technologies

As technology continues to advance at an unprecedented pace, it brings with it a host of new ethical challenges. From AI to biotechnology to virtual reality, new technologies have the power to transform our world in profound ways - but they also come with risks and uncertainties that must be carefully navigated.

This was a topic that had always interested Maya, a young lawyer who had always been passionate about technology and its impact on society. After finishing law school, Maya had worked for a number of different firms, but she had always felt like something was missing. It wasn't until she took a job at a tech startup that she realized what it was: she wanted to help shape the ethical conversation around new technologies.

Over the next few years, Maya worked with her colleagues to create a set of ethical guidelines for their company, outlining the risks and rewards of the technologies they were developing and the potential impact they could have on society. She also worked with other organizations and government agencies to help shape the broader conversation around technology and its impact on society.

As Maya continued to work in this field, she faced a number of challenges along the way. She had to navigate complex legal and regulatory frameworks, as well as ethical dilemmas that arose as a result of new technologies. But through it all, she remained committed to ensuring that the benefits of technology were balanced against the potential risks.

For Maya, the work she did was incredibly rewarding. By helping to shape the ethical conversation around new technologies, she felt like she was making a difference and helping to create a better world for everyone.

CHAPTER FIVE

The Power of Data: Unlocking Insights and Opportunities

Data is a powerful tool that has the potential to unlock new insights and opportunities for growth and innovation. In this chapter, we explore how technology is enabling us to collect, analyze, and use data in new ways, and the impact that this is having on businesses and society as a whole.

We start by looking at the rise of big data and the challenges and opportunities it presents. We examine the various techniques and tools that are available for collecting and analyzing data, and how businesses are using this information to gain insights into their operations and customers.

We also explore the ethical considerations surrounding data collection and use. We examine the importance of data privacy and security, and the need to balance the benefits of data analysis with the risks of misuse or abuse.

Finally, we look at the future of data and how technology is enabling us to collect and analyze data in even more sophisticated ways. From the Internet of Things to machine learning and artificial intelligence, the possibilities for data are endless. We explore the potential of these technologies, and the challenges that must be overcome in order to realize their full potential.

CHAPTER SIX

The Future of Work: Embracing Automation and AI

As automation and artificial intelligence continue to advance, they are transforming the way we work in profound ways. While these technologies have the potential to increase efficiency and productivity, they also raise a number of questions about the future of work and what it means to be a worker in the 21st century.

This is a topic that has always interested Sarah, a young economist who has been studying the impact of automation and AI on the labor market. As she delves deeper into this field, she realizes that the changes are likely to be far-reaching, affecting everything from job availability to the nature of work itself.

Over the next few years, Sarah works with policymakers and businesses to help them understand the implications of these changes. She advocates for policies that support workers and help them adapt to the changing job market, while also exploring new models of work that harness the power of automation and AI.

As Sarah works in this field, she faces a number of challenges along the way. She has to navigate complex economic and social structures, as well as ethical questions about the impact of these technologies on society. But through it all, she remains committed to creating a future of work that is both sustainable and equitable.

CHAPTER SEVEN

The Power of Data: Unlocking the Potential of Big Data and Analytics

Data has always been a powerful tool for businesses, governments, and individuals. But with the advent of big data and analytics, we now have the ability to collect and analyze vast amounts of information in real time, unlocking new insights and opportunities for innovation.

This is a topic that has always fascinated Jack, a young data analyst who has been working with big data and analytics for several years. He sees the potential of these technologies to transform everything from business operations to public policy, and he is eager to help organizations harness the power of data to drive growth and innovation.

Over the next few years, Jack works with a variety of organizations to help them collect, analyze, and apply data in meaningful ways. He develops new tools and techniques for data visualization and analysis, and he helps businesses identify new opportunities for growth and optimization.

As Jack works in this field, he faces a number of challenges, including the need to balance data privacy and security with the benefits of data-driven decision-making. But through it all, he remains committed to using data to unlock the full potential of organizations and create a better future for everyone.

CHAPTER EIGHT

The Future of Education: Using Technology to Create Personalized Learning Experiences

As technology continues to advance, it is transforming the way we learn and engage with information. From online courses to personalized learning platforms, new technologies are making it possible to create learning experiences that are tailored to individual needs and preferences.

This is a topic that has always interested Rachel, a young educator who is passionate about creating engaging and effective learning experiences for students. She sees the potential of technology to transform education and create new opportunities for learning and growth.

Over the next few years, Rachel works with a variety of organizations to help them create personalized learning experiences for students of all ages. She develops new tools and techniques for using technology to engage learners and create interactive learning environments.

As Rachel works in this field, she faces a number of challenges, including the need to balance the benefits of personalized learning with the need for social interaction and hands-on learning experiences. But through it all, she remains committed to using technology to create a more effective and engaging learning environment for everyone.

CHAPTER NINE

The Power of the Crowd: Using Crowdsourcing to Drive Innovation

In recent years, crowdsourcing has emerged as a powerful tool for driving innovation and creativity. From crowdfunding to open innovation platforms, new technologies are making it possible to tap into the collective intelligence of people from around the world to solve complex problems and drive innovation.

This is a topic that has always interested Alex, a young entrepreneur who has been working with crowdsourcing for several years. He sees the potential of these technologies to democratize innovation and create new opportunities for collaboration and creativity.

Over the next few years, Alex works with a variety of organizations to help them harness the power of crowdsourcing to drive innovation. He develops new platforms and techniques for engaging with communities of innovators and creatives, and he helps businesses identify new ideas and opportunities for growth.

As Alex works in this field, he faces a number of challenges, including the need to build trust and create effective incentives for participation. But through it all, he remains committed to using crowdsourcing to create a more inclusive and innovative future for everyone.

CHAPTER TEN

The Future of Humanity: Navigating the Complexities of Technology and Ethics

As technology continues to advance, it is transforming not just the way we live and work, but also the very nature of what it means to be human. From genetic engineering to artificial intelligence, new technologies are raising profound ethical questions about the role of technology in our lives.

This is a topic that has always interested Emma, a young philosopher who has been studying the intersection of technology and ethics for several years. She sees the potential of these technologies to create new opportunities for growth and progress, but also recognizes the need to navigate the complex ethical questions that arise.

Over the next few years, Emma works with a variety of organizations to help them navigate the ethical implications of technology. She develops new frameworks and approaches for thinking about these issues, and she helps businesses and policymakers create policies and guidelines that balance the benefits of technology with the need to protect human values and dignity.

As Emma works in this field, she faces a number of challenges, including the need to balance the demands of innovation with the need for responsible and ethical decision-making. But through it all, she remains committed to using technology to create a more just and equitable world for everyone.

Epilogue

As I conclude this book, "Breaking Boundaries: How Technology is Changing the Game", I am struck by the incredible diversity and complexity of the technological landscape. From artificial intelligence to blockchain, from renewable energy to gene editing, the potential for innovation and disruption is staggering.

Yet amidst this complexity, one thing remains clear: technology is not a force that can be controlled or predicted. It is a constantly evolving ecosystem, shaped by the actions and decisions of countless individuals and organizations around the world. And while there are certainly risks and challenges associated with this level of unpredictability, there is also enormous opportunity for creativity, experimentation, and collaboration.

The stories and insights shared in this book represent just a small fraction of the vast tapestry of technological innovation that is unfolding before us. They are a reminder that the future is not set in stone, and that the choices we make today will shape the world of tomorrow.

So as we move forward into this exciting and uncertain future, I urge you to embrace the power of technology as a tool for positive change. Whether you are an entrepreneur, a policymaker, or simply a curious citizen, you have a role to play in shaping the future of technology.

Thank you for joining me on this journey, and I look forward to continuing the conversation with you.

[Tirth Patel]

Breaking Boundaries: How Technology is Changing the Game book

9 798890 020710

Printed by Libri Plureos GmbH in Hamburg,
Germany